Happy Birthday
Dear Ann

Winston Comes Home

Lob of love
Lucy x

ISBN 978-1-4958-0161-7
ISBN 978-1-4958-0162-4 eBook

Printed in the United States of America

This is a work of fiction. Names, characters, places, and incidents either are the product of the author's imagination or are used fictitiously. Any resemblance to actual events or locales or persons, living or dead, is entirely coincidental.

Published September 2014

INFINITY PUBLISHING
1094 New DeHaven Street, Suite 100
West Conshohocken, PA 19428-2713
Toll-free (877) BUY BOOK
Local Phone (610) 941-9999
Fax (610) 941-9959
Info@buybooksontheweb.com
www.buybooksontheweb.com

Our Story

I was very ill in 2010, a turn in the road that altered the course of the rest of my life, ultimately, for the better; just as my good friend and vet Coral told me it would. When I came out of my recovery and back to life, I was ready to live as much as I could and do all the things I had ever wanted. We never know how long we have, now do we? Just ask a cancer survivor.

One of those things on my life-list was always to have my own horse. I had been a horse maniac all my life, but it had never been the right time, seemingly, to get my own. Sebastian, an amazing white gelding on the Hambey ranch, helped me to get through some really tough days back then, when I was super-sick and anguished. He made me realize that, though I couldn't have him, I had to seize the day and work towards my own.

It happened, amazingly, that we adopted goats – Elvis and Charlie - to eat down our considerable grass and, by chance, they had been living with Winston, the rescue horse whom no one seemed to want. He was a quirky fella, by all accounts, a rescue munchkin from Mexico with more than his fair share of man-made issues. But that didn't scare me a bit. The kind lady who was trying to find him a home told us that no one wanted him. "We do," my husband said and I will never forget how I felt that day. It was practically the day I came back to life.

Though we essentially "rescued" Winston that day and gave him his forever stable in our home we call Solaco; what actually ended up happening was that he rescued us right back. Winston Sebastian Churchill Mason Jensen has given our whole family and extended family so much love, happiness and laughter, that we can no longer imagine how we managed life without him. It seems to me now that he and I had been waiting our whole lives for each other.

This story is dedicated, first and foremost, to his huge and wonderful personality, to Cecilia Ritterbush-Birmingham, who gave us to him in the first place and him to us, Dr. Coral Armstrong who told me it would certainly be this way - and she was right - and to my dear friends and family members, near and far, who helped me come back to life when I needed them most and who have since watched me turn into a happy, fulfilled person, thanks, in part, to my passionate affair with this amazing horse.

Love you all,

Lucy & Winston

Dedication

This story is dedicated to the multitudes of rescue animals who crawl up inside our hearts and stay there for always - also the many brave and wonderful animal rescuers, who will do anything to help a soul from the animal kingdom. All the creatures and characters in this story are real ones and little to no embellishment has been made to create our story.

Thanks must go out to the characters in our story - Elvis, Charlie, Karma, Baxter – and of course Winston - for giving birth to our magical, yet very real, tale.

I hereby pledge to make a donation from every book sold to local animal rescue causes.

Lucy

Winston lived on the Rancho Dominguez; it was all he knew. Horses Gustav, Spirit and baby Chlo all lived on the ranch with him, but they were bullies; especially the bigger horses. Winston was weaker and more timid than them. The other horses would always push in front of him to get to the feed. They would bite him if he tried to edge in and get his share. Sometimes they really hurt him and all he had to eat was the dirt on the ground and muddy water from the ditch. It was all he knew.

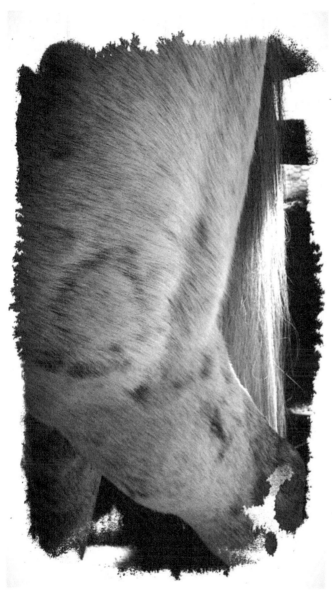

Winston knew that he was always hungry. That much he did know. Sometimes the ranch manager would whip him if he did not go fast enough on the night trips to the border, or tried to snatch some fresh grass along the way to satisfy his constant hunger. The mean manager put a nasty burn on Winston's back leg one time and he did not know why the mean man did that. He hurt Win's feet so badly, when he changed his shoes, that Win would holler and rear. He did not understand why these things were done to him; but it was all he knew.

He would try and talk to the other animals on the ranch. Some were nicer than the mean manager and the mean horses. Karma was the ranch cat and he loved her soft, white nose best of all. She would nuzzle with him in his stable and say, "Don't worry Winston. It won't be forever." He did not know what she meant at the time. He thought she was a very pretty white cat

and that, maybe, one day, they could be married. He was not sure if a horse could marry a cat, but he did like that idea and it made him feel happy.

His friends, the naughty goats, Charlie and Elvis, told him he was a "Silly Billy" to think that way, as they looked for food on the ranch. "Of course a horse can't marry a cat, you stable hound!" Charlie laughed.

But Winston knew inside the depth of his tender feelings for that beautiful white cat, who loved on him more than any other creature he knew and always made him feel better about everything.

But one day Karma did not come and see him. He looked for her up and down the meadow, he looked for her in the feed trough and he looked for her in the stars at night.

He looked in the stable and in the water trough. He looked everywhere. He could not find her. Her words, "It won't be forever" stayed with him and made him sad.

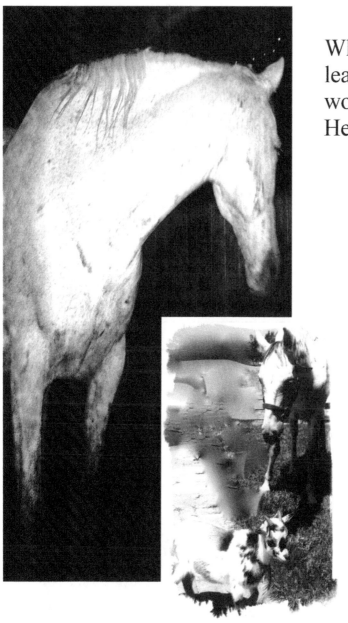

Why, oh why, would she leave him alone in this mean world with these mean folks? He was sad beyond sad.

Even his friend Elvis couldn't cheer him up.

Then one day, a man came to the ranch and started yelling at the mean manager. The mean manager walked up to Winston and grabbed his halter, pulling him across the yard to the horse trailer. "Get in, you no-good horse!" he yelled and he made Winston sad all over again. Sad and very worried. He had always tried to be a good horse. He had tried to please the mean manager, but it had never been enough.

The journey away from the ranch was long and hot and bumpy. Winston shivered with fear in the trailer and could taste the salt of his own sweat. There was only sand to eat in the trailer and he was very afraid. Where was this shouting man taking him? Was there a place out there in the world that was worse than the Rancho Dominguez? He could not imagine that there was, but he was so full of fear he felt sick.

Finally the trailer stopped and a nice lady with a soft voice helped him out. He was so tired that he did not have the strength to show his fear to her.

He was very thirsty from all that driving and had nasty dust in his throat and all over his body. The lady led him to the meadow and he rolled his body in the cool grass and drank the ice cold water.

He wondered where he was and where he would have to go next. Why would nobody love him and keep him forever like some of the other horses he had known on the Rancho Dominguez? That made him sad, because he had always tried to be a sweet boy and not bite and buck and be a bully like the others.

He looked to the skies for answers and hoped that Karma was there listening to him and helping him to find his way through to where she was; a place where they could be together again.

He closed his eyes and tried to dream the way.

Then he heard a shout. "Winning, you made it!" It was a goat noise that he had heard somewhere before. The next thing he knew, those naughty goats came running up the hill at him, banging their horns together in their race to reach him first. It was Charlie and Elvis from the Rancho Dominguez.

They had arrived at this place before him! He hugged those crazy guys, as much as a horse can hug two sets of moving horns - without stepping on them or getting stabbed.

He had so many questions he could hardly stand himself. What was this place? What was it like and would they be able to stay there together forever?

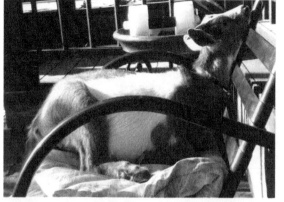

"Oh yes, we will. We three are brothers; we will always be together!" said Charlie, as he rested in the lounge chair. Charlie always had something to say. "This is the bestest place in the whole world. They give you two meals a day and often snacks too. The water is fresh and they never kick us! We can just run around all day and play and be happy!"

"Bestest is not a word," Elvis chimed in, also seated on a patio chair and ever the smarty pants.

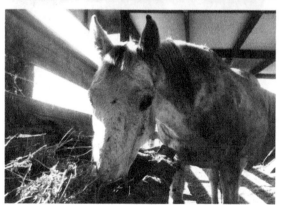

"They won't be planning on cooking you?" asked Winston, ever cautious about terrible things he had seen in his terrible past, as he tucked into his evening meal.

"No, we don't think so", the goats chattered on, grazing close by with their happy banter Winston had missed so much.

"They build us fires here only to make us warm and play us music to make us happy. The dogs and cats here are really friendly too.

Sometimes we even get to run around the swimming pool, eat tomatoes and play musical chairs!" Charlie added. "The lady makes us toast in the morning as well!"

"That does sound like fun," Winston said dubiously, wondering what his own place would be in this strange new place.

He had never been kissed and hugged before by a human and it felt strange, but good. The lady brushed him, fed him and cleaned his feet. Then she hugged him again.

It was then that the nice lady came out and put her arms around him, kissing the still tender bite marks on his neck. "I love you, Winston Sebastian Churchill Mason Jensen," she said, giving him a really long name that he had never heard before. "You are home now, in your forever home, and no one will hurt you again."

"See!" said Elvis from his position in the stable trough. "You will be staying in the bestest place in the world too. We'll all be staying in it together."

"Bestest is not a word," teased Charlie and off they went, bouncing down the hill and fight-playing like brothers do.

The old ginger dog on the ranch, Baxter, nodded at Winston through the fence, in greeting. "Welcome to Solace, Bud," he said and went about his business. "You'll like it here," he glanced back. "You will. We all do."

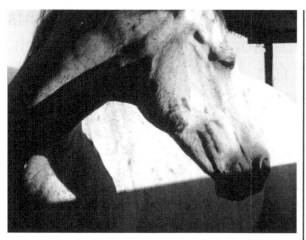 

Winston looked out over the meadow of his new home to the fields in the valley below and wondered what the future would bring. He was still anxious; he was always anxious and could not stop the tremble in his mouth, nor his fear about when his next meal would be.

But, at least, he felt calmer now he was reunited with his two friends, the goats from the old country. He was also just a little bit hopeful about his new home in this new world.

Behind him, a rainbow streamed across the sky, as if to say "Welcome home, Winston."

Already the Rancho Dominguez seemed a long way away. He would no longer have to be hungry again, it seemed. He would no longer have to be afraid, or cold. Nothing would come to bite him or harm him or burn him. He would be able to sleep in peace without being woken up to go on a scary night trip to the border, or by the bite of another horse, because he was in the wrong place at the wrong time. He stood at the gate of his new stable in his new life and he did feel as if he had really, finally, come home.

Maybe, in time, he would learn to love the hugs and kisses of the nice lady, not be afraid of them. Maybe, in time, he might even be able to give her some back.

Baxter, the old ginger dog, poked his brindle muzzle again through the fence and commented, "None of us who come here, Bud, ever plan to leave." It was as if he had read his mind. Winston felt a well of happiness gush from his heart.

Winston went to sleep that night on the new straw of the new stable of his new life and slept peacefully for a very long time; longer than he could ever remember.

Somewhere in his dreams a soft white cat came to him and said, "See Winston. I told you it wouldn't be forever," as she lay at his hooves, purring, just like she always did.

When he woke up, he was not sure if his sweetheart Karma had really been there with him or not.

In any case, he woke up feeling happy and better and ready for a wonderful day in the meadow with his old friends and his new feeling of peace.

Thanks

Trough loads of thanks must go out to all who helped this story come together! To my human family, who have always supported, and, in some cases, shared my passion: Marc, Adam, Francoise and Mike. Thank you for loving my "Winning Boy" nearly as much as I do!

To my dear friends, Carey and Kate, who helped me with editing and photos and wonderful ideas, not to mention encouragement – forever friends for always! I love you so much.

To the Central Coast Writer's Group that consistently gave me food for thought and helped push me and my project along to completion; you were always worth the hour journey there and the hour back to give me inspiration.

To my publisher, Infinity Publishing, thank you for making the process a little less painful and the end result a piece I can be proud of. LUnabooks was lucky to find you and become your publishing partner.

To all the amazing animal rescue groups and individuals out there who share my same passion – I pledge a donation from every book sold will be donated to local animal rescue causes. Last, but most certainly not least, to my wonderful farm of rescue characters, babies of my heart – I adore all of you and I am so glad that you found me. I hope, in time, to be able to write all of your stories.

And to my dear, darling Winston, thank you for all you have given me. You have climbed up into my soul with those big old feet of yours and I shall love you eternally.

Lucy

"When you see Lucy and Winston together, you know that those two were waiting their whole lives to find each other. The backwards and forwards comfort and trust that flows between them is tangible, and one can only look on and smile."

- Carey

A few words from friends and family about our main man, our "Winning Boy", Winston Sebastian Churchill Mason Jensen, the white rescue horse from Mexico, who has changed many lives and continues to surprise and amuse us every day.

"To me, Winston was the cure for cancer. Though the drugs and all did their part, it was not until Winston came to live with us that I really saw my wife come back to life and to living."

- Mike

- *"I sometimes wondered if Winston was half mule as he could be so stubborn! I was told his kick could snap my leg and that was the last time I attempted to lift his back hooves."* - Sheryl (quoted after a rainy winter holiday she spent on our ranch when Winston wouldn't let her clean his feet!)

- *"I have had the privilege of knowing Winston from his early days at Solace, where he arrived, afraid of so much, emotionally battered and physically scarred from his former life. What joy to watch his happy journey to become the confident King of the Ranch he now is, his huge spirit unbroken. Lucky me to have galloped through the vineyards on him and along the sands of the Monterey Bay. He's a powerful horse with a great big heart and is a wonderful testimony to the healing power of love and devotion."* - Kate

---

- *"Winston, "Winning", my noble steed, my love, my wonderful friend. How lucky am I that you came into my life with all your edges and bumps and bruises. Scarred and grey together, we were quite the pair and remain so. I rescued you and you rescued me right back. We are pieces of each other's puzzle. I couldn't love you more. Every day I can't wait to see you all over again. "* - Lucy

CPSIA information can be obtained at www.ICGtesting.com
Printed in the USA
BVOW10s1820201014

371331BV00003B/1/P